HAL•LEONARD

T0068325

VOLUME 58
2nd Edition

bruno mars

Cover photo: Pg/ mediapunch

To access audio visit:
www.halleonard.com/mylibrary

Enter Code
2681-1723-9226-9632

ISBN 978-1-4950-2833-5

HAL•LEONARD®
CORPORATION
7777 W. BLUEMOUND RD. P.O. BOX 13819 MILWAUKEE, WI 53213

In Australia Contact:
Hal Leonard Australia Pty. Ltd.
4 Lentara Court
Cheltenham, Victoria, 3192 Australia
Email: ausadmin@halleonard.com.au

Visit Hal Leonard Online at
www.halleonard.com

Grenade

**Words and Music by Bruno Mars, Ari Levine, Philip Lawrence,
Brody Brown, Claude Kelly and Andrew Wyatt**

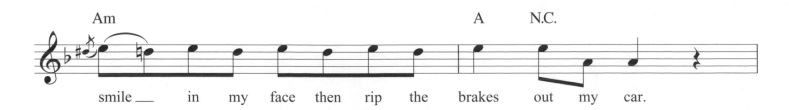

smile __ in my face then rip the brakes out my car.

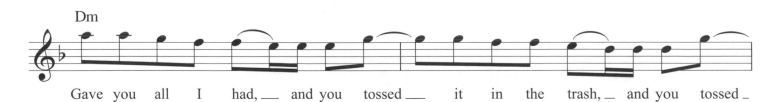

Gave you all I had, __ and you tossed __ it in the trash, __ and you tossed __

__ it in the trash, yes, you did. __ To give __ me all your love __ is all __

__ I ev - er asked, __ 'cause __ what you don't un-der-stand __ is, I'd catch a gre-nade __

⊕ Coda
Bridge

If my bod - y was on fi - re, oo, you'd

watch me burn down in flames. You said you loved me; you're a li - ar, 'cause you

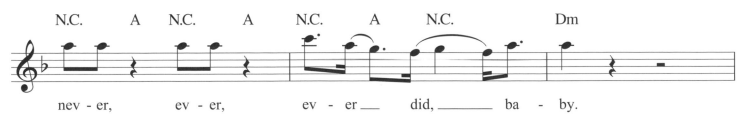

nev - er, ev - er, ev - er __ did, _____ ba - by.

But dar - lin', I'd still catch a gre - nade __

Chorus

___ for ya, _____ throw my hand on a blade ___ for ya, _____

I'd jump in front of a train ___ for ya, ___ you know I'd do an-y-thing ___

___ for ya. ___ Oo, _____ I would go through all ___ this pain, _

_____ take a bul-let straight through my brain. _____ Yes, I would die _

Outro

___ for you, ba - by, but you won't do the same,

no, you won't do ___ the same. _ You would-n't do ___ the same. _

_____ Woo, ___ you'll nev - er do ___ the same. _

___ No, _____ no, no, no. _____

Just the Way You Are

Words and Music by Bruno Mars, Ari Levine, Philip Lawrence, Khari Cain and Khalil Walton

Intro
Moderately

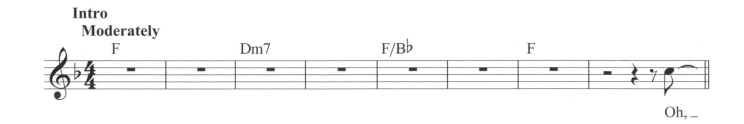

Oh, __

Verse

__ her eyes, her eyes make the stars look __ like they're __ not shin - in',

her hair, __ her hair falls per - fect - ly __ with - out __ her try - ing,

she's so __ beau - ti - ful, __ and I tell her ev - 'ry __

__ day. __ Yeah, I know, I know when I

com - pli - ment __ her, she won't be - lieve me, it's so, it's so sad to

think that she — don't see — what I see, but ev-'ry time — she ask — me, "Do —

— I look — o - kay?" — I say: _____ When I see your face, —

Chorus

— there's not a thing — that — I — would change, —

— 'cause you're a - maz - ing just — the — way — you are. —

And when you smile, —

the whole world stops — and — stares — for a while, — 'cause girl, you're a - maz -

To Coda

- ing just — the — way — you are. —

Verse

Yeah. — Her lips, — her lips I could

Girl, you're a - maz - ing just ___

___ the ___ way ___ you are. ___ When I see your face, ___

Outro-Chorus

___ there's not a thing ___ that ___ I ___ would change, ___

___ 'cause you're a - maz - ing just ___ the ___ way ___ you are. ___

And when you smile, ___

the whole world stops ___ and stares ___ for a while, ___ 'cause girl, you're a - maz -

- ing ___ just ___ the ___ way ___ you are. ___

Yeah. ___

The Lazy Song

Words and Music by Bruno Mars, Ari Levine, Philip Lawrence and Keinan Warsame

Chorus

Outro

Locked Out of Heaven

**Words and Music by Bruno Mars,
Ari Levine and Philip Lawrence**

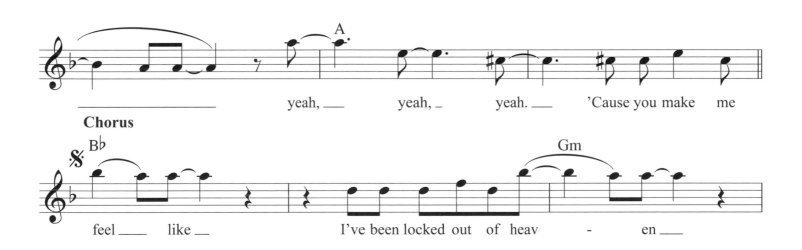

can't wait to see the light.

And right there is where I want to stay, ee -

ay - ee - ay. 'Cause your sex takes me to par - a - dise, yeah, your sex

takes me to par - a - dise. And it shows,

D.S. al Coda

yeah, yeah, yeah. 'Cause you make me

Coda

Bridge

Oh,

yeah. Can I just stay here,

1.

spend the rest of my days here?

Marry You

Words and Music by Bruno Mars, Ari Levine and Philip Lawrence

Verse

Well, I know this lit-tle chap-el on the boul-e-vard. We can

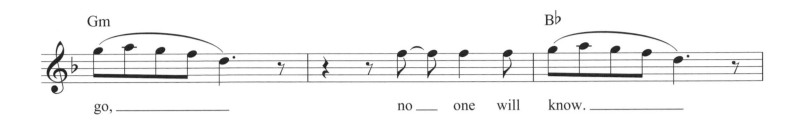

go, _____ no __ one will know. _____

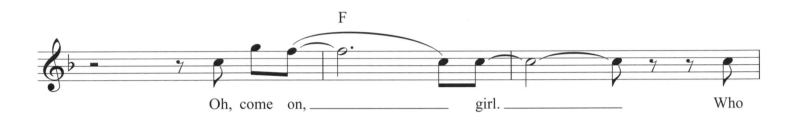

Oh, come on, _____ girl. _____ Who

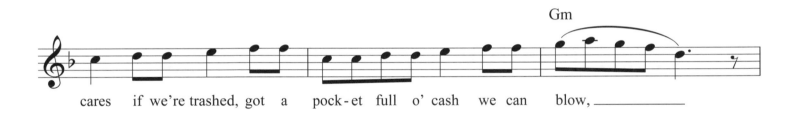

cares if we're trashed, got a pock-et full o' cash we can blow, _____

shots _ of Pa - trón, _____ and it's on, _

_____ girl. __ Don't say no, no, no, no, no, __ just say

Pre-chorus

yeah, yeah, yeah, yeah, yeah, __ and we'll go, go, go, go, go, _

if you're read - y   like I'm read - y.   'Cause it's a

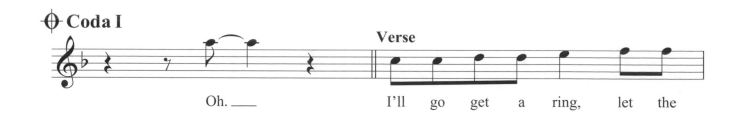
Oh. ___   I'll   go   get   a   ring,   let   the

cho - ir bells sing like "oo," ___   so what - cha wan - na

do? ___   Let's just run, ___ girl. __

If we wake up, and you wan - na break up, that's   cool, ___

no, I ___ won't blame you, ___   it was fun, __

___ girl. __   Don't say   no, no, no, no, no, __

20

just say yeah, yeah, yeah, yeah, yeah, ___ and we'll go, go, go, go, go, ___ if you're read - y like I'm read-

⊕ Coda II

D.S. al Coda II

Bridge

- y. 'Cause it's a   Just say, ___ "I do." _____

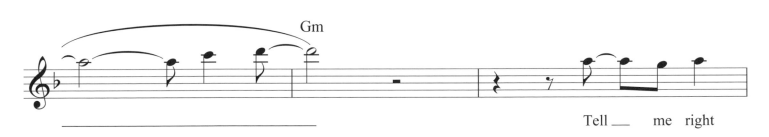

Tell ___ me right

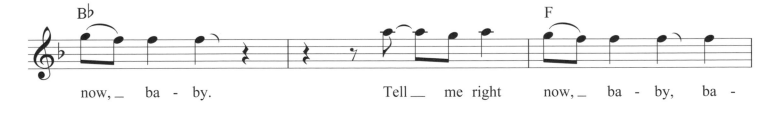

now, ___ ba - by.   Tell ___ me right   now, ___ ba - by, ba -

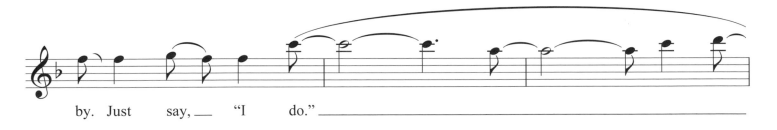

by. Just say, ___ "I do." _____

Tell ___ me right   now, ___ ba - by.

Tell __ me right now, __ ba - by, ba - by. Oh, __ it's a

Chorus

beau - ti - ful night, __ we're look- in' for __ some-thin' dumb to do. __

Hey, ba - by, ____ I think I wan - na mar - ry you. __

__ Is it the look in your eyes, __

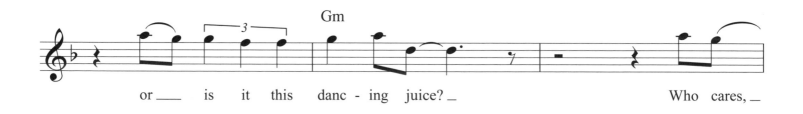

or __ is it this danc - ing juice? __ Who cares, __

__ ba - by? I think I wan - na mar - ry you. _____

Treasure

**Words and Music by Bruno Mars, Ari Levine,
Philip Lawrence, Fredrick Brown, Thibaut Berland and Christopher Acito**

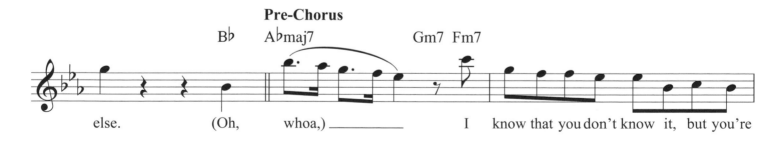

fine, so fine. _ (Fine, so fine. _ Oh, whoa,) _____ oh,

girl, I'm gon - na show you when you're mine, all mine. _

Chorus

(Mine, all mine.) _ Treas-ure. That is what you are. _

_____ Hon- ey, you're my gold - en star, and if you can make _

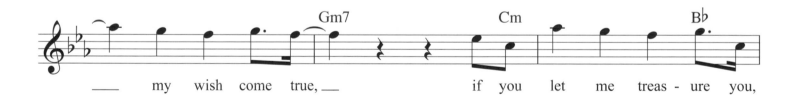

_____ my wish come true, _ if you let me treas - ure you,

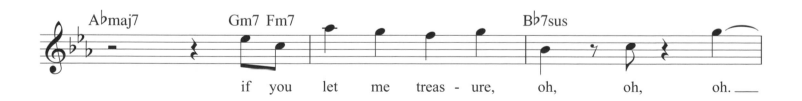

if you let me treas - ure, oh, oh, oh. _

Verse

_____ Pret - ty girl, pret - ty girl, pret - ty girl, you should be smil-

24

- in'.   A   girl   like   you   should   nev - er   look   so

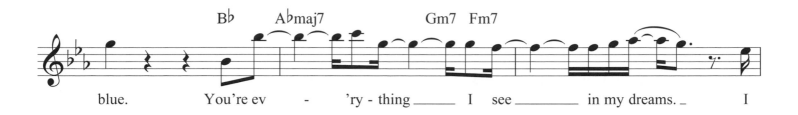

blue.   You're ev -   'ry - thing _____ I   see _____ in my dreams. _   I

would - n't   say   that   to   you   if   it   was - n't   true.   (Oh,

Pre-Chorus

whoa,) _____   I   know   that   you   don't know   it,   but you're

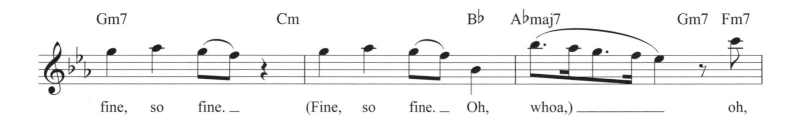

fine,   so   fine. _   (Fine,   so   fine. _   Oh,   whoa,) _____   oh,

girl, I'm gon - na show you when you're mine,   all   mine. _   (Mine,   all   mine.) _

𝄋 Chorus

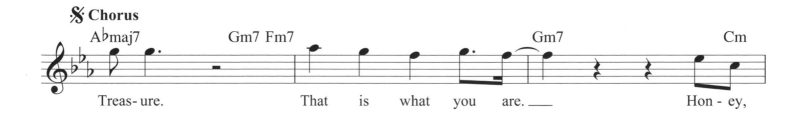

Treas - ure.   That   is   what   you   are. ____   Hon - ey,

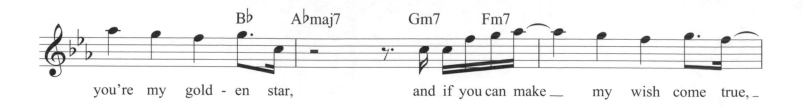

you're my gold - en star, and if you can make __ my wish come true, __

__ if you let me treas - ure you, if you

let me treas - ure, oh, oh, oh. ___

Bridge

You are my treas - ure, you are my treas - ure, you are my treas - ure, yeah,

you, you, you, you are. You are my treas - ure, you are my treas - ure,

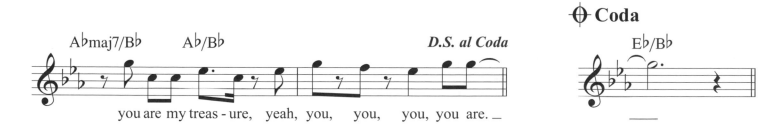

you are my treas - ure, yeah, you, you, you, you are. __

Outro

26

Uptown Funk

**Words and Music by Mark Ronson, Bruno Mars,
Philip Lawrence, Jeff Bhasker, Devon Gallaspy and Nicholaus Williams**

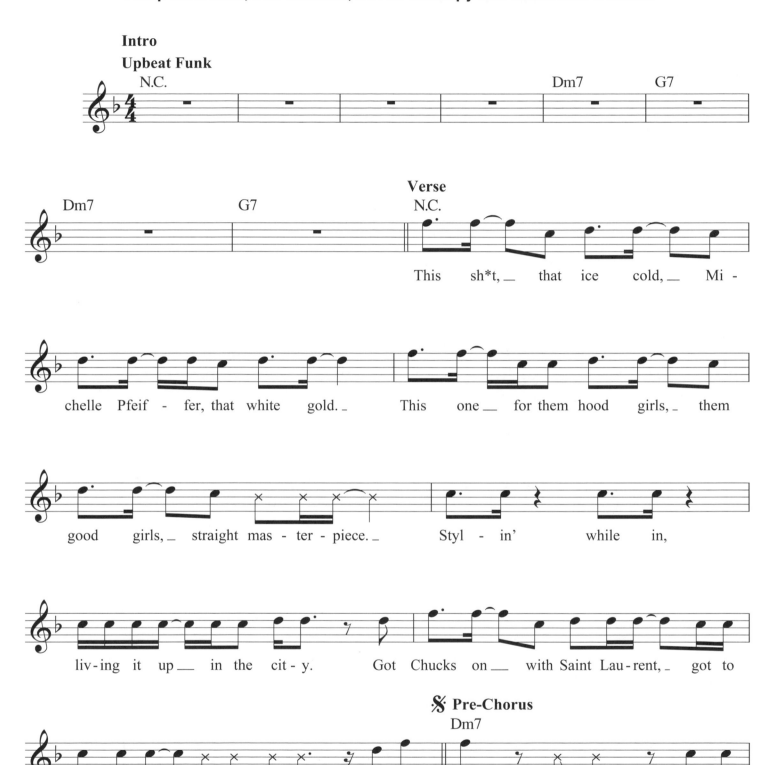

po - lice _ and a fi - re - man. _ I'm too hot. (Hot damn.) Make a

drag - on want _ to re - ti - re, man. _ I'm too hot. (Hot damn.)

Say my name, _ you know who I am. _ I'm too hot. (Hot damn.) Am I

Chorus

bad 'bout _ that mon - ey? Break it down. Girls hit _ you, hal - le - lu - jah.

Girls hit _ you, hal - le - lu - jah. Girls hit _ you, hal - le - lu - jah. 'Cause

up - town funk gon' give it to you. ('Cause up - town funk gon' give it to you.) 'Cause

up - town funk gon' give it to you. Sat - ur - day night _ and we in the spot. _

Interlude

Don't be - lieve _ me? Just watch. Come on.

Don't be-lieve — me? Just watch.

Don't be-lieve — me? Just watch.   Don't be-lieve — me? Just watch.

To Coda ⊕

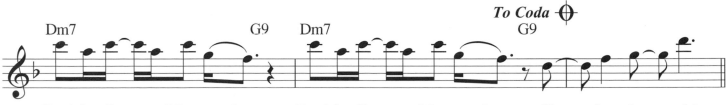

Don't be-lieve — me? Just watch. —   Don't be-lieve — me? Just watch. —   Hey, — hey, hey, — oh!

Bridge

Stop,   wait a min-ute,   fill my cup, — put some li-quor in it.

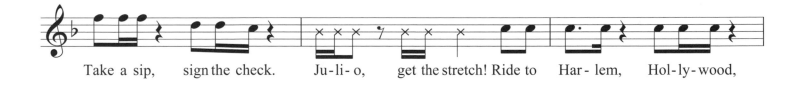

Take a sip,   sign the check. Ju-li-o,   get the stretch! Ride to Har-lem,   Hol-ly-wood,

Jack-son, — Mis-sis-sip-pi.   If we show up, — we gon-na show out,

D.S. al Coda   ⊕ **Coda**

smooth-er than a fresh jar of Skip-py.   I'm too   — hey, hey, — oh!

Bridge

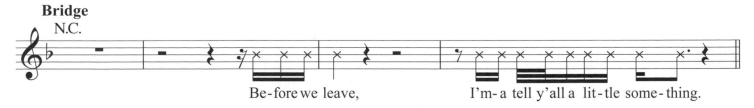

Be-fore we leave,   I'm-a tell y'all a lit-tle some-thing.

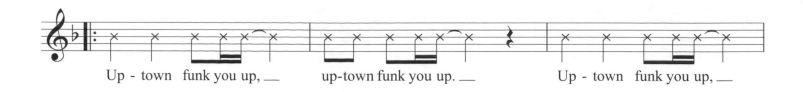

Up - town funk you up, __ up-town funk you up. __ Up - town funk you up, __

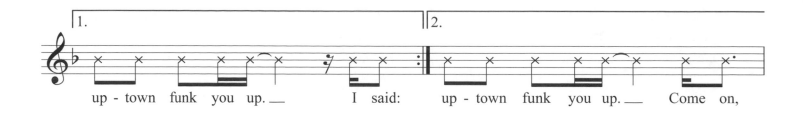

1.
up - town funk you up. __ I said: 2. up - town funk you up. __ Come on,

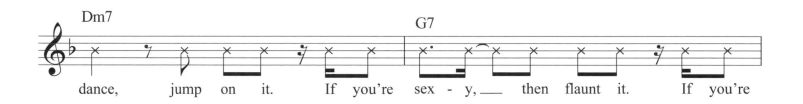

Dm7   G7
dance, jump on it. If you're sex - y, __ then flaunt it. If you're

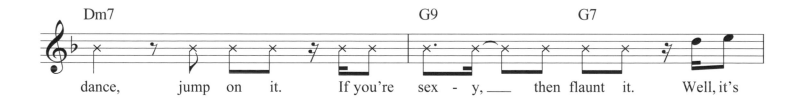

Dm7   G7   G9
freak - y, __ then own it. Don't brag a - bout __ it, come show me. Come on,

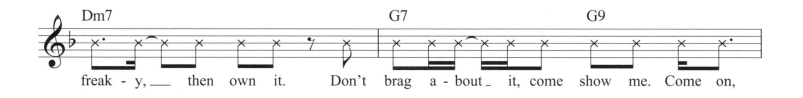

Dm7   G9   G7
dance, jump on it. If you're sex - y, __ then flaunt it. Well, it's

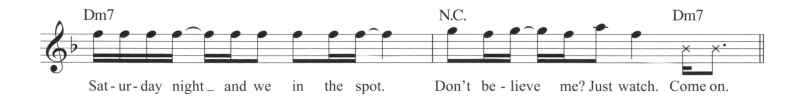

Dm7   N.C.   Dm7
Sat - ur - day night __ and we in the spot. Don't be - lieve me? Just watch. Come on.

Interlude

G9   Dm7

30

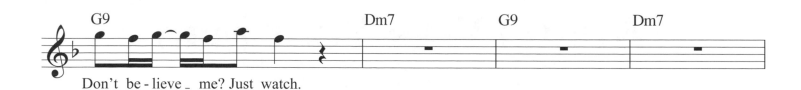

Don't be - lieve _ me? Just watch.

Don't be - lieve _ me? Just watch.   Don't be - lieve _ me? Just watch.

Don't be - lieve _ me? Just watch. _   Don't be - lieve _ me? Just watch. _   Hey, _

Outro

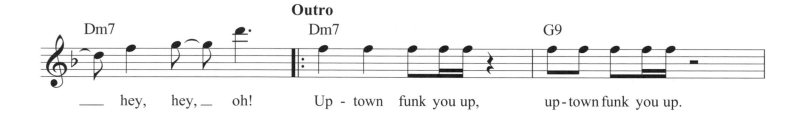

_ hey, hey, _ oh!   Up - town funk you up,   up - town funk you up.

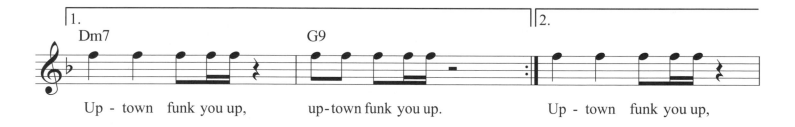

Up - town funk you up,   up - town funk you up.   Up - town funk you up,

up - town funk you up.   Come on!   Up - town funk you up,   up - town funk you up.

Up-town funk you up,   up-town funk you up.   Up-town funk you up.

When I Was Your Man

**Words and Music by Bruno Mars, Ari Levine,
Philip Lawrence and Andrew Wyatt**

**Intro
Soulful**

Verse

Same bed, but it feels just a lit-tle bit big - ger now.

Our song on the ra - di - o, but it don't sound the same.

When our friends talk a-bout you, all it does is just tear me down,

'cause my heart breaks a lit-tle when I hear your name. It all just sounds like

Pre-Chorus

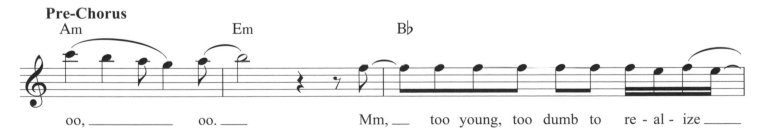

oo, oo. Mm, too young, too dumb to re-al-ize

Chorus

C/G   G   N.C.   F   G

___ that I ___ should-'ve bought you flow - ers ___ and held your hand. _

C

_____ Should - 've gave you all my ho - urs ___ when I had _ the _

C   F   G

___ chance. Take _ you to ev - 'ry par - ty, 'cause all _ you want - ed to do ___ was dance. _

Am7   D7   Dm   Fm

_3_

_____ Now ___ my ba-by's danc - in', _ but she's danc- in' with an-oth-er man. _

Verse

C   F   C   G/B   Am   C

___ Uh. My pride, my e - go, my needs, and my self -

Dm   G

- ish ways _ caused a good, strong wom-an like you to walk out _

C   Em/B   Am   C

_3_

___ my life. _ Now I nev-er, ___ nev - er got to clean up the mess _

Dm   G

_3_

___ I _ made, _ oh, _____ and it haunts me ev-'ry time I close ___

33

C   Em/B   **Pre-Chorus**   Am   Em

— my eyes. — It all just sounds like oo, ———— oo. —— Mm, ——

B♭   C/G   G   N.C.

— too young, too dumb to re-al-ize ——— that I —— should-'ve bought you flow-

Chorus

F   G   C

- ers ——— and held your hand. ——— Should-'ve gave you all my ho-

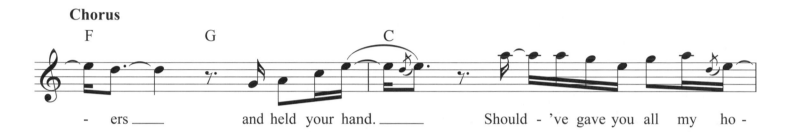

F   G   C

- urs ——— when I had — the — chance. Take — you to ev-'ry par-

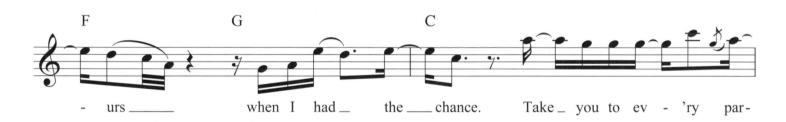

F   G   Am7   D7

- ty, 'cause all — you want-ed to do — was dance. ——————— Now —— my ba-by's danc-

Dm   Fm   C

- in', — but she's danc-in' with an-oth-er man. — Al-though it

Bridge

F   G

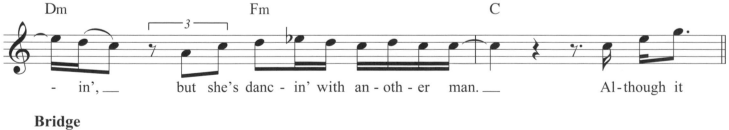

hurts, — I'll be the — first ————— to say — that I was

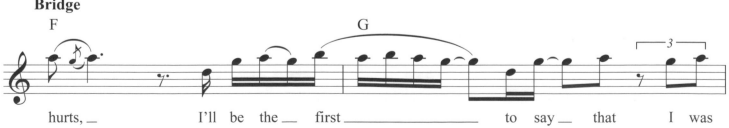

Pro Vocal® Series
SONGBOOK & SOUND-ALIKE AUDIO
SING GREAT SONGS WITH A PROFESSIONAL BAND

Whether you're a karaoke singer or an auditioning professional, the Pro Vocal® series is for you! Unlike most karaoke packs, each book in the Pro Vocal Series contains the lyrics, melody, and chord symbols for at least eight hit songs. The audio contains demos for listening, and separate backing tracks so you can sing along. The CD is playable on any CD player, but it is also enhanced so PC and Mac computer users can adjust the recording to any pitch without changing the tempo! Perfect for home rehearsal, parties, auditions, corporate events, and gigs without a backup band.

<table>
<tr><td colspan="2">WOMEN'S EDITIONS</td></tr>
<tr><td>00740247</td><td>1. Broadway Songs.....................$14.95</td></tr>
<tr><td>00740249</td><td>2. Jazz Standards.......................$15.99</td></tr>
<tr><td>00740246</td><td>3. Contemporary Hits...............$14.95</td></tr>
<tr><td>00740277</td><td>4. '80s Gold.................................$12.95</td></tr>
<tr><td>00740299</td><td>5. Christmas Standards............$15.95</td></tr>
<tr><td>00740281</td><td>6. Disco Fever............................$12.95</td></tr>
<tr><td>00740279</td><td>7. R&B Super Hits.....................$12.95</td></tr>
<tr><td>00740309</td><td>8. Wedding Gems.......................$12.95</td></tr>
<tr><td>00740409</td><td>9. Broadway Standards.............$14.95</td></tr>
<tr><td>00740348</td><td>10. Andrew Lloyd Webber...........$14.95</td></tr>
<tr><td>00740344</td><td>11. Disney's Best..........................$15.99</td></tr>
<tr><td>00740378</td><td>12. Ella Fitzgerald........................$14.95</td></tr>
<tr><td>00740350</td><td>14. Musicals of Boublil & Schönberg..$14.95</td></tr>
<tr><td>00740377</td><td>15. Kelly Clarkson.......................$14.95</td></tr>
<tr><td>00740342</td><td>16. Disney Favorites...................$15.99</td></tr>
<tr><td>00740353</td><td>17. Jazz Ballads...........................$14.99</td></tr>
<tr><td>00740376</td><td>18. Jazz Vocal Standards...........$17.99</td></tr>
<tr><td>00740354</td><td>21. Jazz Favorites.......................$14.99</td></tr>
<tr><td>00740374</td><td>22. Patsy Cline.............................$14.95</td></tr>
<tr><td>00740369</td><td>23. Grease....................................$14.95</td></tr>
<tr><td>00740367</td><td>25. Mamma Mia............................$15.99</td></tr>
<tr><td>00740365</td><td>26. Movie Songs.........................$14.95</td></tr>
<tr><td>00740363</td><td>29. Torch Songs..........................$14.95</td></tr>
<tr><td>00740379</td><td>30. Hairspray...............................$15.99</td></tr>
<tr><td>00740380</td><td>31. Top Hits.................................$14.95</td></tr>
<tr><td>00740384</td><td>32. Hits of the '70s....................$14.95</td></tr>
<tr><td>00740388</td><td>33. Billie Holiday.........................$14.95</td></tr>
<tr><td>00740389</td><td>34. The Sound of Music.............$16.99</td></tr>
<tr><td>00740390</td><td>35. Contemporary Christian.......$14.95</td></tr>
<tr><td>00740392</td><td>36. Wicked...................................$17.99</td></tr>
<tr><td>00740396</td><td>39. Christmas Hits......................$15.95</td></tr>
<tr><td>00740410</td><td>40. Broadway Classics...............$14.95</td></tr>
<tr><td>00740415</td><td>41. Broadway Favorites.............$14.99</td></tr>
<tr><td>00740416</td><td>42. Great Standards You Can Sing......$14.99</td></tr>
<tr><td>00740417</td><td>43. Singable Standards..............$14.99</td></tr>
<tr><td>00740418</td><td>44. Favorite Standards..............$14.99</td></tr>
<tr><td>00740419</td><td>45. Sing Broadway......................$14.99</td></tr>
<tr><td>00740420</td><td>46. More Standards.....................$14.99</td></tr>
<tr><td>00740421</td><td>47. Timeless Hits........................$14.99</td></tr>
<tr><td>00740422</td><td>48. Easygoing R&B......................$14.99</td></tr>
<tr><td>00740424</td><td>49. Taylor Swift...........................$16.99</td></tr>
<tr><td>00740426</td><td>51. Great Standards Collection.............$19.99</td></tr>
<tr><td>00740430</td><td>52. Worship Favorites................$14.99</td></tr>
<tr><td>00740434</td><td>53. Lullabyes...............................$14.99</td></tr>
<tr><td>00740438</td><td>54. Lady Gaga..............................$14.99</td></tr>
<tr><td>00740444</td><td>55. Amy Winehouse....................$15.99</td></tr>
<tr><td>00740445</td><td>56. Adele.....................................$16.99</td></tr>
<tr><td>00740446</td><td>57. The Grammy Awards Best Female Pop Vocal Performance 1990-1999..$14.99</td></tr>
<tr><td>00740447</td><td>58. The Grammy Awards Best Female Pop Vocal Performance 2000-2009..$14.99</td></tr>
<tr><td>00109374</td><td>60. Katy Perry.............................$14.99</td></tr>
<tr><td>00116334</td><td>61. Taylor Swift Hits..................$14.99</td></tr>
<tr><td>00123120</td><td>62. Top Downloads.....................$14.99</td></tr>
</table>

<table>
<tr><td colspan="2">MEN'S EDITIONS</td></tr>
<tr><td>00740250</td><td>2. Jazz Standards.......................$14.95</td></tr>
<tr><td>00740298</td><td>5. Christmas Standards............$15.95</td></tr>
<tr><td>00740280</td><td>6. R&B Super Hits.....................$12.95</td></tr>
<tr><td>00740411</td><td>9. Broadway Greats..................$14.99</td></tr>
<tr><td>00740333</td><td>10. Elvis Presley – Volume 1.................$14.95</td></tr>
<tr><td>00740349</td><td>11. Andrew Lloyd Webber...........$14.99</td></tr>
<tr><td>00740347</td><td>13. Frank Sinatra Classics.........$14.95</td></tr>
<tr><td>00740334</td><td>14. Lennon & McCartney............$14.99</td></tr>
<tr><td>00740453</td><td>15. Queen.....................................$14.99</td></tr>
<tr><td>00740335</td><td>16. Elvis Presley – Volume 2.................$14.99</td></tr>
<tr><td>00740351</td><td>18. Musicals of Boublil & Schönberg..$14.95</td></tr>
<tr><td>00740337</td><td>19. Lennon & McCartney – Volume 2...$14.99</td></tr>
<tr><td>00740346</td><td>20. Frank Sinatra Standards.......$14.95</td></tr>
<tr><td>00740338</td><td>21. Lennon & McCartney – Volume 3...$14.99</td></tr>
<tr><td>00740358</td><td>22. Great Standards...................$14.99</td></tr>
<tr><td>00740336</td><td>23. Elvis Presley.........................$14.99</td></tr>
<tr><td>00740341</td><td>24. Duke Ellington.......................$14.99</td></tr>
<tr><td>00740339</td><td>25. Lennon & McCartney – Volume 4..$14.99</td></tr>
<tr><td>00740359</td><td>26. Pop Standards......................$14.99</td></tr>
<tr><td>00740362</td><td>27. Michael Bublé.......................$15.99</td></tr>
<tr><td>00740454</td><td>28. Maroon 5...............................$14.99</td></tr>
<tr><td>00740364</td><td>29. Torch Songs..........................$14.95</td></tr>
<tr><td>00740366</td><td>30. Movie Songs.........................$14.95</td></tr>
<tr><td>00740368</td><td>31. Hip Hop Hits.........................$14.95</td></tr>
<tr><td>00740370</td><td>32. Grease....................................$14.95</td></tr>
<tr><td>00740371</td><td>33. Josh Groban..........................$14.95</td></tr>
<tr><td>00740373</td><td>34. Billy Joel...............................$14.99</td></tr>
<tr><td>00740382</td><td>36. Hits of the '60s....................$14.95</td></tr>
<tr><td>00740385</td><td>38. Motown..................................$14.95</td></tr>
<tr><td>00740386</td><td>39. Hank Williams........................$14.95</td></tr>
<tr><td>00740387</td><td>40. Neil Diamond.........................$14.95</td></tr>
<tr><td>00740391</td><td>41. Contemporary Christian.......$14.95</td></tr>
<tr><td>00740397</td><td>42. Christmas Hits......................$15.95</td></tr>
<tr><td>00740399</td><td>43. Ray...$14.95</td></tr>
<tr><td>00740400</td><td>44. The Rat Pack Hits.................$14.99</td></tr>
<tr><td>00740401</td><td>45. Songs in the Style of Nat "King" Cole$14.99</td></tr>
<tr><td>00740402</td><td>46. At the Lounge.......................$14.95</td></tr>
<tr><td>00740403</td><td>47. The Big Band Singer.............$14.95</td></tr>
<tr><td>00740404</td><td>48. Jazz Cabaret Songs..............$14.99</td></tr>
<tr><td>00740405</td><td>49. Cabaret Songs......................$14.99</td></tr>
<tr><td>00740412</td><td>51. Broadway's Best...................$14.99</td></tr>
<tr><td>00740427</td><td>52. Great Standards Collection...$19.99</td></tr>
<tr><td>00740431</td><td>53. Worship Favorites................$14.99</td></tr>
<tr><td>00740435</td><td>54. Barry Manilow......................$14.99</td></tr>
<tr><td>00740436</td><td>55. Lionel Richie.........................$14.99</td></tr>
<tr><td>00740439</td><td>56. Michael Bublé – Crazy Love.........$15.99</td></tr>
<tr><td>00740441</td><td>57. Johnny Cash..........................$14.99</td></tr>
<tr><td>00740442</td><td>58. Bruno Mars............................$14.99</td></tr>
<tr><td>00740448</td><td>59. The Grammy Awards Best Male Pop Vocal Performance 1990-1999..$14.99</td></tr>
<tr><td>00740449</td><td>60. The Grammy Awards Best Male Pop Vocal Performance 2000-2009..$14.99</td></tr>
<tr><td>00740452</td><td>61. Michael Bublé – Call Me Irresponsible.....................$14.99</td></tr>
</table>

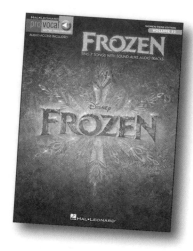

<table>
<tr><td>00101777</td><td>62. Michael Bublé – Christmas.............$19.99</td></tr>
<tr><td>00137717</td><td>63. Jersey Boys...........................$14.99</td></tr>
<tr><td>00109288</td><td>64. Justin Bieber.........................$14.99</td></tr>
<tr><td>00123119</td><td>65. Top Downloads.....................$14.99</td></tr>
</table>

EXERCISES

<table>
<tr><td>00123770</td><td>Vocal Exercises.........................$14.99</td></tr>
<tr><td>00740395</td><td>Vocal Warm-Ups........................$14.99</td></tr>
</table>

MIXED EDITIONS

These editions feature songs for both male and female voices.

<table>
<tr><td>00740311</td><td>1. Wedding Duets......................$12.95</td></tr>
<tr><td>00740398</td><td>2. Enchanted..............................$14.95</td></tr>
<tr><td>00740407</td><td>3. Rent...$14.95</td></tr>
<tr><td>00740408</td><td>4. Broadway Favorites..............$14.99</td></tr>
<tr><td>00740413</td><td>5. South Pacific..........................$15.99</td></tr>
<tr><td>00740429</td><td>7. Christmas Carols...................$14.99</td></tr>
<tr><td>00740437</td><td>8. Glee...$16.99</td></tr>
<tr><td>00740443</td><td>10. Even More Songs from Glee...........$15.99</td></tr>
<tr><td>00116960</td><td>11. Les Misérables......................$19.99</td></tr>
<tr><td>00126476</td><td>12. Frozen...................................$19.99</td></tr>
</table>

KIDS EDITIONS

<table>
<tr><td>00740451</td><td>1. Songs Children Can Sing!................$14.99</td></tr>
</table>

Visit Hal Leonard online at
www.halleonard.com

HAL•LEONARD®
7777 W. BLUEMOUND RD. P.O. BOX 13819 MILWAUKEE, WI 53213

Disney characters and artwork © Disney Enterprises, Inc.

Prices, contents, & availability subject to change without notice.

1214

ORIGINAL KEYS FOR SINGERS

Titles in the Original Keys for Singers series are designed for vocalists looking for authentic transcriptions from their favorite artists. The books transcribe famous vocal performances exactly as recorded and provide piano accompaniment parts so that you can perform or pratice exactly as Ella or Patsy or Josh!

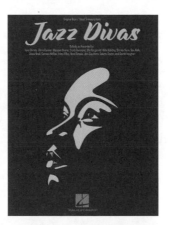

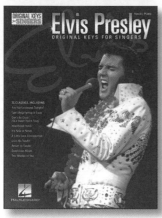

ACROSS THE UNIVERSE
00307010...$19.95

LOUIS ARMSTRONG
00307029...$19.99

THE BEATLES
00307400...$19.99

BROADWAY HITS (FEMALE SINGERS)
00119085...$19.99

BROADWAY HITS (MALE SINGERS)
00119084...$19.99

MARIAH CAREY
00306835...$19.95

PATSY CLINE
00740072...$18.99

ELLA FITZGERALD
00740252...$17.99

JOSH GROBAN
00306969...$19.99

GREAT FEMALE SINGERS
00307132...$19.99

GREAT MALE SINGERS
00307133...$19.99

BILLIE HOLIDAY
Transcribed from Historic Recordings
00740140...$17.99

JAZZ DIVAS
00114959...$19.99

LADIES OF CHRISTMAS
00312192...$19.99

NANCY LAMOTT
00306995...$19.99

LEONA LEWIS – SPIRIT
00307007...$17.95

CHRIS MANN
00118921...$16.99

MEN OF CHRISTMAS
00312241...$19.99

THE BETTE MIDLER SONGBOOK
00307067...$19.99

THE BEST OF LIZA MINNELLI
00306928...$19.99

ONCE
00102569...$16.99

ELVIS PRESLEY
00138200...$19.99

SHOWSTOPPERS FOR FEMALE SINGERS
00119640...$19.99

BEST OF NINA SIMONE
00121576...$19.99

FRANK SINATRA – MORE OF HIS BEST
00307081...$19.99

TAYLOR SWIFT
00142702...$16.99

STEVE TYRELL – BACK TO BACHARACH
00307024...$16.99

THE BEST OF STEVE TYRELL
00307027...$16.99

SARAH VAUGHAN
00306558...$17.95

VOCAL POP
00312656...$19.99

ANDY WILLIAMS – CHRISTMAS COLLECTION
00307158...$17.99

ANDY WILLIAMS
00307160...$17.99

HAL•LEONARD® CORPORATION

7777 W. BLUEMOUND RD. P.O. BOX 13819 MILWAUKEE, WI 53213

www.halleonard.com

Prices, contents, and availability subject to change without notice.

0615